G000296026

Bradshaw's Railway
Diary 2017

This diary belongs to

....

1 - 6 Jan.
14 - 31 March.
5 - 12 May
30 June - 14 July.
22 Sept - 29 Sept
27 Oct - 3 Nov.

Published in Great Britain in 2016 by Old House books & maps
(part of Bloomsbury publishing Plc)
c/o Osprey Publishing, PO Box 883, Oxford OX2 9PH, UK.
c/o Osprey Publishing, 1385 Broadway, Fifth Floor New York,
NY 10018, USA.
Website: www.oldhousebooks.co.uk

© 2016 Old House
All rights reserved. Apart from any fair dealing for the purpose
of private study, research, criticism or review, as permitted
under the Copyright, Designs and Patents Act, 1988, no part
of this publication may be reproduced, stored in a retrieval
system, or transmitted in any form or by any means, electronic,
electrical, chemical, mechanical, optical, photocopying,
recording or otherwise, without the prior written permission
of the copyright owner. Enquiries should be addressed to the
Publishers. Every attempt has been made by the Publishers to
secure the appropriate permissions for materials reproduced in
this book. If there has been any oversight we will be happy to
rectify the situation and a written submission should be made
to the Publishers.

A CIP catalogue record for this book is available from the
British Library.
ISBN-13: 978 1 78366 056 8
Compiled by Nicholas Wright.

Cover Images: Left, the Midland Hotel, Manchester
(Mary Evans); middle, GWR Locomotive No. 16 *Brunel* of 1894
(Stuart Black); right, London's King's Cross Station in 1908
(Mary Evans).

Title page image: London, Brighton & South Coast
Railway trains at Victoria Station, London, *c.* 1887.
(Past Pix/SSPL/Getty)

'Diary belongs to' image: The Great Hall, Euston Square
Station, in 1849. This building, along with Euston's great
'Doric Portico', was destroyed by British Rail in 1960–1. (Print
Collector/Getty)

Printed in China through World Print Ltd.
16 17 18 19 20   10 9 8 7 6 5 4 3 2 1

CALENDAR 2017

January
M	T	W	T	F	S	S
						1
2	3	4	5	6	7	8
9	10	11	12	13	14	15
16	17	18	19	20	21	22
23	24	25	26	27	28	29
30	31					

February
M	T	W	T	F	S	S
		1	2	3	4	5
6	7	8	9	10	11	12
13	14	15	16	17	18	19
20	21	22	23	24	25	26
27	28					

March
M	T	W	T	F	S	S
		1	2	3	4	5
6	7	8	9	10	11	12
13	14	15	16	17	18	19
20	21	22	23	24	25	26
27	28	29	30	31		

April
M	T	W	T	F	S	S
					1	2
3	4	5	6	7	8	9
10	11	12	13	14	15	16
17	18	19	20	21	22	23
24	25	26	27	28	29	30

May
M	T	W	T	F	S	S
1	2	3	4	5	6	7
8	9	10	11	12	13	14
15	16	17	18	19	20	21
22	23	24	25	26	27	28
29	30	31				

June
M	T	W	T	F	S	S
			1	2	3	4
5	6	7	8	9	10	11
12	13	14	15	16	17	18
19	20	21	22	23	24	25
26	27	28	29	30		

July
M	T	W	T	F	S	S
					1	2
3	4	5	6	7	8	9
10	11	12	13	14	15	16
17	18	19	20	21	22	23
24	25	26	27	28	29	30
31						

August
M	T	W	T	F	S	S
	1	2	3	4	5	6
7	8	9	10	11	12	13
14	15	16	17	18	19	20
21	22	23	24	25	26	27
28	29	30	31			

September
M	T	W	T	F	S	S
				1	2	3
4	5	6	7	8	9	10
11	12	13	14	15	16	17
18	19	20	21	22	23	24
25	26	27	28	29	30	

October
M	T	W	T	F	S	S
						1
2	3	4	5	6	7	8
9	10	11	12	13	14	15
16	17	18	19	20	21	22
23	24	25	26	27	28	29
30	31					

November
M	T	W	T	F	S	S
		1	2	3	4	5
6	7	8	9	10	11	12
13	14	15	16	17	18	19
20	21	22	23	24	25	26
27	28	29	30			

December
M	T	W	T	F	S	S
				1	2	3
4	5	6	7	8	9	10
11	12	13	14	15	16	17
18	19	20	21	22	23	24
25	26	27	28	29	30	31

CALENDAR 2018

January
M	T	W	T	F	S	S
1	2	3	4	5	6	7
8	9	10	11	12	13	14
15	16	17	18	19	20	21
22	23	24	25	26	27	28
29	30	31				

February
M	T	W	T	F	S	S
			1	2	3	4
5	6	7	8	9	10	11
12	13	14	15	16	17	18
19	20	21	22	23	24	25
26	27	28				

March
M	T	W	T	F	S	S
			1	2	3	4
5	6	7	8	9	10	11
12	13	14	15	16	17	18
19	20	21	22	23	24	25
26	27	28	29	30	31	

April
M	T	W	T	F	S	S
						1
2	3	4	5	6	7	8
9	10	11	12	13	14	15
16	17	18	19	20	21	22
23	24	25	26	27	28	29
30						

May
M	T	W	T	F	S	S
	1	2	3	4	5	6
7	8	9	10	11	12	13
14	15	16	17	18	19	20
21	22	23	24	25	26	27
28	29	30	31			

June
M	T	W	T	F	S	S
				1	2	3
4	5	6	7	8	9	10
11	12	13	14	15	16	17
18	19	20	21	22	23	24
25	26	27	28	29	30	

July
M	T	W	T	F	S	S
						1
2	3	4	5	6	7	8
9	10	11	12	13	14	15
16	17	18	19	20	21	22
23	24	25	26	27	28	29
30	31					

August
M	T	W	T	F	S	S
		1	2	3	4	5
6	7	8	9	10	11	12
13	14	15	16	17	18	19
20	21	22	23	24	25	26
27	28	29	30	31		

September
M	T	W	T	F	S	S
					1	2
3	4	5	6	7	8	9
10	11	12	13	14	15	16
17	18	19	20	21	22	23
24	25	26	27	28	29	30

October
M	T	W	T	F	S	S
1	2	3	4	5	6	7
8	9	10	11	12	13	14
15	16	17	18	19	20	21
22	23	24	25	26	27	28
29	30	31				

November
M	T	W	T	F	S	S
			1	2	3	4
5	6	7	8	9	10	11
12	13	14	15	16	17	18
19	20	21	22	23	24	25
26	27	28	29	30		

December
M	T	W	T	F	S	S
					1	2
3	4	5	6	7	8	9
10	11	12	13	14	15	16
17	18	19	20	21	22	23
24	25	26	27	28	29	30
31						

EUSTON SQUARE STATION - LONDON & NORTH WESTERN RAILWAY

Passing under the magnificent Doric entrance, which forms so grand a feature of the metropolitan terminus of this line of railway, the huge pile of building at once arrests the eye. It was designed by Philip Hardwick, Esq., and erected by Messrs. William Cubitt and Co., at a cost of about £150,000.

This hall for size and grandeur is probably unique; in dimensions it is truly gigantic, being 125 feet in length, 61 feet in width, and 60 feet in height. At the northern end is a noble flight of steps, leading to a vestibule, in which are doors entering into the general meeting room, the board room, and the conference room, and the gallery which runs around the hall, thus giving facility of communication to an infinity of offices connected with the railway traffic.

The style of architecture is Roman ionic, and has been treated with great skill. The bas reliefs which adorn the panels in the corners of the hall are eight in number, and typify the chief cities and boroughs with which the North Western Railway communicates. They are London, Liverpool, Manchester, Birmingham, Carlisle, Chester, Lancaster and Northampton.

The large group in alto-relievo over the door leading to the general meeting room, is an extremely picturesque and effective composition – representing Britannia, supported by Science and Industry. The statue of the late George Stephenson, who effected more than any other engineer has done towards the development of the railway system, is a very appropriate ornament to the great hall.

Bradshaw's Handbook, 1863.

Boxing Day (bank holiday, UK)	Monday **26**
Bank holiday (UK)	Tuesday **27**
	Wednesday **28**
	Thursday **29**
	Friday **30**
	Saturday **31**
New Year's Day	Sunday **1**

A contemporary watercolour by an unknown artist of the grand Doric propylaeum of Euston station, with its flanking lodges. Designed by Philip Hardwick, it was one of the great landmarks of London. (SSPL/Getty)

The London & North Western Railway had at its core some of the earliest and most important mainline routes in England, and liked to refer to itself as the 'Premier Line'. This early twentieth century poster shows the LNWR network, and illustrates a number of the places that could be reached by train from the company's Euston terminus, as well as some of the sights en route. (SSPL/Getty)

Bank holiday (UK)

Monday

2

Bank holiday (Scotland)

Tuesday

3

Wednesday

4

Thursday

5

Friday

6

Saturday

7

Sunday

8

Monday

9

Tuesday

10

Wednesday

11

Thursday

12

Friday

13

Saturday

14

Sunday

15

LNWR porters load passengers' belongings into a luggage van for the journey north at Euston Station, c. 1900. (SSPL/Getty)

WOLVERTON - LONDON & NORTH WESTERN RAILWAY

Wolverton, near the river Ouse, has an increasing population of 2,370, chiefly dependent on the London and North Western Railway Company, who have a depot and extensive factories here. It is also a refreshment station. A new church and market house, and hundreds of model cottages, have been built by the company, whose works cover 12 acres of ground. While Crewe is the nursery, Wolverton is the hospital for locomotives. There are the worn-out, the ricketty, the accidents, and sundry other wards, in all of which locomotives are to be seen undergoing cure. Red hot pieces of iron are being forcibly administered; holes probed and nuts screwed on them; steam lathes are facing down callosities; hundreds of locomotive surgeons – stalwart and iron-fisted – dress and bind up cases in their wards

with a tremendous energy. Sickly-looking locomotives are fitted up with bran (sic) new outsides; several in the last stages of collapse have strong doses of copper rivets forced into their systems. Metal giants, shaky about the knees, are furnished with new sets of joints. In the most desperate cases a cure is effected. Ninety-nine out of every hundred of these battered patients come out perfectly restored to their bereaved stokers. By the help of a blast furnace and steam hammer, even the most incurable is beaten young again, and reproduced as a new locomotive, called perhaps the "Phoenix" – (*Household Words*, 1853.) Nothing is wasted here, for the scraps are welded together in the furnace, for axles or cranks, or any other duty requiring temper or strength. The metal cutting and planing works deserve notice.

Bradshaw's Handbook, 1863.

Monday

16

Tuesday

17

Wednesday

18

Thursday

19

Friday

20

Saturday

21

Sunday

22

An express passenger locomotive of the LNWR undergoing maintenance at Wolverton in 1852, as depicted in the
Illustrated London News. *(SSPL/Getty)*

Monday

23

Tuesday

24

Burns' Night

Wednesday

25

Thursday

26

Friday

27

Saturday

28

Sunday

29

Giving the right away. A guard of the London & North Western Railway signals to the driver that his train is ready to depart, c. 1905. (SSPL/Getty)

STRATFORD-UPON-AVON - GREAT WESTERN RAILWAY

This interesting part of Warwickshire is directly accessible by a branch of the Oxford, Worcester, and Wolverhampton line, by which means it is within 100 miles journey by rail from London. A Roman road, called the Fossway, crossed the river at this point, and hence the name. It is a municipal borough but derives its chief importance from being the birthplace of Shakespeare, who was born here on 23rd April (St. George's day), 1564, in an old-fashioned timbered house, opposite the Falcon, in Henley Street, which, after some changes, and the risk even of being transferred as it stood to America, by a calculating speculator, was at last purchased by the Shakespeare Club, and adopted by Government as a tribute to his memory.

Stratford-upon-Avon,
 "Where his first infant lays sweet Shakespeare sung,
 Where the last accents faltered on his tongue,"

And to which the genius of one man has given immortality, is situated on a gentle ascent from the river Avon in the county of Warwick. If the visitor ascends the uplands on the high road to Warwick, he will behold a panorama of remarkable richness and variety. Hill and dale in graceful undulations – luxuriant wooded parks – the winding Avon tracked by the fringe of willows on its banks – the peaceful town and its venerable church – and afar off, the gradually towering outline of the Malvern hills form, altogether, a landscape essentially English, and such as is rarely to be found in any other country than our own. But rich and pleasant as the prospect is, it takes its crowning glory from the immortal poet, the mighty genius whose dust reposes at our feet. It is his genial spirit which pervades and sanctifies the scene; and every spot on which the eye can rest claims some association with his life. We tread the very ground a thousand times, and feel as he has felt.

Bradshaw's Handbook, 1863.

Monday

30

Tuesday

31

Wednesday

1

Thursday

2

Friday

3

Saturday

4

Sunday

5

Painted in 1859, Charles Rossiter's *To Brighton and Back for 3 shillings and sixpence* shows third class railway travel as the writer of *Bradshaw's Handbook* would have observed it. (Universal History Archive/Getty)

Monday
6

Tuesday
7

Wednesday
8

Thursday
9

Friday
10

Saturday
11

Sunday
12

BIRMINGHAM NEW STREET STATION - LONDON & NORTH WESTERN RAILWAY

The progressive extension of the railway system led to the erection of several buildings for its general purposes; and these structures are entitled to rank amongst the most stupendous architectural works of the age.

Situated in New Street, Birmingham, the entrance is at the bottom of Stephenson Place, through an arcade, to the booking offices for the respective railways; passing through these we emerge on a magnificent corridor or gallery, guarded by a light railing, and open to the station (but enclosed by the immense glass and iron roof), from whence broad stone staircases, with bronze rails, afford access to the departure platform. We then stand on a level with a long series of offices, appropriated to the officials of the company, and a superb refreshment room, divided into three portions by rows of massive pillars, annexed to which is an hotel (the Queen's).

The interior of this station deserves attention from its magnitude. The semicircular roof is 1,100 feet long, 205 feet wide, and 80 feet high, composed of iron and glass, without the slightest support except that afforded by the pillars on either side. If the reader notice the turmoil and bustle created by the excitement of the arrival and departure of trains, the trampling of crowds of passengers, the transport of luggage, the ringing of bells, and the noise of two or three hundred porters and workmen, he will retain a recollection of the extraordinary scene witnessed daily at the Birmingham Central Railway Station.

Bradshaw's Handbook, 1863.

Monday

13

Valentine's Day   Tuesday

14

Wednesday

15

Thursday

16

Friday

17

Saturday

18

Sunday

19

This late-nineteenth-century photograph of light and airy New Street will not ring any bells for modern users of this station. (SSPL/Getty)

Monday

20

Tuesday

21

Wednesday

22

Thursday

23

Friday

24

Saturday

25

Sunday

26

Wearing a tall top hat typical of the period, Mr Widdowson, a pay clerk of the LNWR, stands by a locomotive and its crew at around the time that Bradshaw's Handbook *was written. (SSPL/Getty)*

DUDLEY AND THE BLACK COUNTRY - GREAT WESTERN RAILWAY

—◌ • ◌—

Dudley is a borough town in the county of Worcester. It received its name from a celebrated Saxon chieftain, who, as early as the year 700, built the castle which now commands the town.

The night view from Dudley Castle of the coal and iron districts of South Staffordshire reminds the spectator of the Smithy of Vulcan, described by Homer. The lurid flames that issue from the summits of the huge columnar chimneys light up the horizon for miles around, and impart to every object a gloomy aspect. On whichever side the view is taken in open day, the evidences of mining industries present themselves, in the vast number of smoking, fiery and ever-active works, which teem in this part of South Staffordshire. Taking Dudley Castle as a centre, we have to the north Tipton, Gornal, Sedgley, Bilston, Wolverhampton, Willenhall, and Wednesfield. More easterly we find Great Bridge, Toll End, Darlaston, Wednesbury, West Bromwich, and Swan Village, which is a similar group to the former, and marked with precisely the same features – mining perforations, red brick houses, and black smoke. Turning towards the south, we find the iron towns fewer and wider apart, and lying, as it were, confusedly in four counties – Birmingham, for instance, in Warwickshire; Smethwick, Dudley Port, Rowley Regis, Wordsley, and Kingswinford in Staffordshire; Oldbury, Hales Owen, Dudley, and Stourbridge, in Worcestershire. So singular, indeed, is the intersection of these four counties that in going from Birmingham to Dudley Castle, by way of Oldbury – a distance of about eight miles by coach road – we pass out of Warwick into Staffordshire, thence into Worcester, and a third time into Staffordshire, for although Dudley town is in Worcestershire, Dudley Castle and grounds are in Staffordshire. These several towns belong to the mining and manufacturing district, known by the name of the South Staffordshire *coal field* district, because it has a layer of coal running, so far as is known, beneath its surface.

Dudley Castle belongs to Lord Ward, who is also proprietor of a considerable portion of Dudley and its mines. It is situated in a large and highly picturesque park; and, with its warders' watch and octagon towers, triple gate, keep, vault, and dungeon, dining and justice halls, and chapel, though in a state of dilapidation, must be considered as a fine old ruin. The view from the summit of the keep is wide-spreading and singularly interesting; to the north-east you have Lichfield cathedral; to the east, the busy hive of Birmingham; whilst to the south-west, nature has formed the Malvern Hills. These objects are all visible, and form an interesting background to the environs of Dudley.

As the eye sweeps the horizon from the summit of the keep of Dudley Castle, to discern the precise character of each object and locality, the mind is struck with one particular fact,

A prospect of the landscape around Wolverhampton, drawn for the Illustrated London News *in the 1860s, gives a sense of the extraordinary density of industry in this region. (Hulton Archive/Getty)*

GREAT WESTERN RAILWAY.

ART AND INDUSTRIAL EXHIBITION AT WOLVERHAMPTON

MAY to NOVEMBER 1902.

CHEAP TICKETS. **EXCURSION TRAINS.**

Full particulars at the Stations and Offices of the Company

PADDINGTON STATION. APRIL. 1902.   J.L.WILKINSON, General Manager.

that almost every town, village, house, man, woman, child, every occupation and station, are more or less dependent on, and are at the mercy of, lumps of coal and iron, and that the human race will mainly owe their moral regeneration to these two materials. The miner digs, the roaster calcines, the smelter reduces, the founder casts, the blacksmith forges, and the whitesmith files; these are but parts of the vast hive, whose busy hum of industry is heard far and wide, and whose skillful handiworks find a ready reception in every quarter of the globe. Leave Birmingham to itself, and direct your eye to West Bromwich – which itself sprung up as it were but yesterday – and there you will perceive the best *puddlers* at work – the converters of pig-iron into its barred state – by far the most important of all the processes in the manufacture of that metal. Wolverhamption, Wednesbury, Bilston, and Dudley, have each their respective industries and carry the division of labour to the minutest degree. Bloxwich, is almost entirely employed in making awl-blades and bridle-bits; Wednesfield keeps to its locks, keys, and traps; Darlaston its gun locks, hinges and stirrups; Walsall its buckles, spurs and bits; Wednesbury its gas-pipes, coach springs, axles, screws, hinges and bolts; Bilston its japan-work and tin-plating; Sedgley and its neighbourhood, its nails; Willenhall its locks, keys, latches, curry-combs, bolts and grid-irons; Dudley its vices, fire-irons, nails and chains; Tipton its heavy iron-work; while Wolverhampton includes nearly all these employments in metal work. Looking further south, there may be descried Oldbury, Smethwick, Rowley Regis, Hales Owen, and Stourbridge – all of which are engaged in some form or another, in the manufacture of iron. We have not space to enlarge upon these facts, which are only a few in the vast multitude that are comprised in the area over which the view from the castle extends, and therefore must content ourselves with laying a single one before the reader. The quantity of cast-iron produced throughout England and Scotland in 1851, amounted to nearly three millions of tons, and the share in that production by this district may be estimated at about one third of that quantity, or five millions in value. Assuredly this limited area presents the most remarkable concentration of industry of which the world can boast.

Bradshaw's Handbook, 1863.

An early twentieth-century poster published by the Great Western Railway, advertising an exhibition of the wares of this key industrial region. (SSPL/Getty)

STOKE-ON-TRENT - NORTH STAFFORDSHIRE RAILWAY

This is the busy capital of the *Staffordshire Potteries*, a district 9 miles long, including *Longton, Fenton, Burslem, Etruria, Tunstall,* &c., which, with the other places, are incorporated within the new borough, containing a population of 101,207, who return two members, nearly all employed in the manufacture of pottery, or the arts connected with it. Potters' clay (though of a coarse quality) and coal are both abundant; hence the peculiar advantages hitherto possessed by this spot. Stout low kilns, like the martello towers in Kent, are smoking about everywhere; each the centre of a pottery establishment, for which a "Bank" is the local name. Copeland's Bank, for instance, means Copeland's Works. At these, and at Minton's are produced the most beautiful porcelain, rivalling the best made abroad; also the terracotta, tessellated tiles, &c., so extensively used in new churches, and the small figures, in imitation of marble statuary.

At Stoke, the principal buildings are, a modern *Town Hall*, vast *Railway Station*, built in the Tudor style, at a cost of £150,000. The approaches are paved with Minton's tiles; new *Church*, in which are the tombs of Wedgwood and Spode, two eminent names in this locality. Wedgwood died in 1795, at Etruria, so called because of his successful imitation of the ancient vases under that name, now the seat of one of his family. At *Stoke*, or *Fenton Manor House*, Fenton, the poet, was born. Dr Lightfoot the Hebraist, was a native. Hanley and Longton are both larger than Stoke. Peacock coal is quarried at the former, and at the latter much of the coarser sort of pottery is made.

When the staple manufacture and the people have been thoroughly examined, there is little else attractive in this important quarter, although the scenery is not altogether void of interest. It is well provided with railways and canals. The first sod of the Grand Trunk Canal was cut by Wedgwood himself; and the North and South Staffordshire railways have been opened since 1847, having been amalgamated with the canal.

Bradshaw's Handbook, 1863.

Monday

27

Tuesday

28

St David's Day

Wednesday

1

Thursday

2

Friday

3

Saturday

4

Sunday

5

NORTHWICH -
MANCHESTER, SHEFFIELD
AND LINCOLNSHIRE
RAILWAY

Northwich is the principal seat of the salt trade. The salt is worked either in the mines, 200 or 300 feet deep, under the gypsum, or produced from the brine springs. One of the largest, the *Marston or Dale's Mine*, should be visited by the curious traveller, descended in three or four minutes by a shaft 250 feet deep, to the excavated chambers below, spread over 35 acres, the sparkling roof being supported by great solid salt columns 60 feet square. When Canning visited the mine, it was lit up with thousands of candles and blue lights, producing a most brilliant effect. The rock salt is variegated and dirty-looking, and was first found in searching for coal; which, according to geological rule, may be reached some hundreds of feet lower. That from the springs is evaporated in immense iron pans; at Droitwich 260,000 tons are annually made in this way. About twice as much more is produced by the rock mines. The Nantwich trade has declined.

Bradshaw's Handbook, 1863.

Monday
6

Tuesday
7

Wednesday
8

Thursday
9

Friday
10

Saturday
11

Sunday
12

An early-nineteenth century coloured aquatint engraving showing the underground chamber of a Cheshire salt mine, illustrating the pillars of salt left in place to support the ceiling. (SSPL/Getty)

Printed early in the twentieth century to promote tourism in Derbyshire, this poster illustrates some of the sights visible or accessible from the Midland Railway's main line through what is described in *Bradshaw's Handbook* as 'one of the most enchanting districts in the world, unsurpassable in boldness, grandeur, and magnificence of character'. (SSPL/Getty)

Monday

13

Tuesday

14

Wednesday

15

Thursday

16

St Patrick's Day (bank holiday, NI)

Friday

17

Saturday

18

Sunday

19

The writer of *Bradshaw's Handbook* warned readers of the treacherous quicksands at Morecambe, but in this early twentieth century poster, the LNWR were happy to entice juvenile cricketers to the resort as a suitable place to pursue their passion. (SSPL/Getty)

Monday
20

Tuesday
21

Wednesday
22

Thursday
23

Friday
24

Saturday
25

Mothering Sunday

Sunday
26

The Caledonian, which fancied itself as supreme in Scotland as the LNWR did in England, continued the so-called West Coast main line north of the border. This early-twentieth-century map shows the Caledonian network and its connections. (SSPL/Getty)

Monday
27

Tuesday
28

Wednesday
29

Thursday
30

Friday
31

Saturday
1

Sunday
2

ST ANDREWS - NORTH BRITISH RAILWAY

St Andrews is of so much historical celebrity, and so rich in memorials of the past, that no one can say he has seen Scotland who has not paid it a visit. Dr. Johnson was here in 1773, in his tour with Boswell; in its streets, "there is," says he "the silence and solitude of inactive indigence and gloomy depopulation" – a truly Johnsonian burst. Unfortunately it stands out of the beaten track. Something, however, has been done to redeem its neglected air, by a townsman, Major Andrews, who, while provost, exerted himself to stop the progress of decay, and introduced modern improvements. There are three principal streets, most of the houses of which are large and antique-looking; at the end of one, on the west side of the town, is an old gate, a remnant of the walls which surrounded it.

Three colleges compose the *University*, which was founded in 1411, by Bishop Wardlaw. *St. Salvador* (or Saviour's) is an unfinished quadrangle, 230 feet long, begun by Bishop Kennedy, whose effigies are in the chapel. *St. Leonard's* was founded by Prior Hepburn in 1552; there is an old ruined Gothic church attached to it, and a modern one by the side. The third is *St. Mary's*, which has been lately restored. About 150 students frequent this University. The library contains upwards of 50,000 volumes.

The harbour is rocky, and of little consequence. Formerly it had good trade. One branch of manufacture still flourishes here, that of making balls for golf – a favourite game, played in the links or flat sands along the sea shore.

Bradshaw's Handbook, 1863.

Monday

3

Tuesday

4

Wednesday

5

Thursday

6

Friday

7

Saturday

8

Sunday

9

Monday

10

Tuesday

11

Wednesday

12

Thursday

13

Good Friday (bank holiday, UK)

Friday

14

Saturday

15

Easter Sunday

Sunday

16

A happy (and well-to-do) Edwardian family embark on their holidays. (Ullstein Bild/Getty)

Sir Walter Scott was a heroic figure for Victorian and Edwardian Britons, and this poster entices lovers of his writing to visit the Scotland that inspired him. Published by the Caledonian's great east coast rivals, the North British Railway, this poster was anxious to stress the luxury of its services, which included on-board lavatories. (SSPL/Getty)

Easter Monday (bank holiday, UK exc. Scotland)

Monday

17

Tuesday

18

Wednesday

19

Thursday

20

Friday

21

Saturday

22

St George's Day

Sunday

23

ABERDEEN - SCOTTISH NORTH EASTERN RAILWAY

Aberdeen (New), the capital of the county, is considered the third city of importance in Scotland. It lies on a slightly elevated ground on the north bank of the river Dee, near the efflux into the sea, and about a mile and a half from the mouth of the Don. It is a large and handsome city, having many spacious streets, lined on each side by elegant houses, built of granite from the neighbouring quarries.

Aberdeen derives its name from the Dee, on the north bank of which it lies, not far from the *Devana* of Ptolemy, and the river's mouth (*"aber"* in Gaelic), which makes an excellent port, whence cotton, linen, woolen goods, combs, and writing papers, in large quantities, granite, cattle, and agricultural produce from the interior, salmon, &c., are exported in great quantities. The salmon is sent to Billingsgate Market packed in ice, an ingenious plan for preserving it, which was first adopted here. The fisheries on the Dee, worth £10,000 a-year to the city, were originally granted by Bruce, on account of the gallant behaviour of the people in driving out the English garrison planted here by Edward I. Their watch-word was "Bon-Accord," which is the motto of Aberdeen to this day. A history of the town has been written under this title. Its harbour, improved by Telford at a great cost, contains 34 acres, the pier is 1,200 feet long. Recently a large wet dock has been constructed, for the shipping of which there are registered at the port 230, nearly 70,000 tonnage.

Besides cotton and woollen mills, ironworks and ship-yards, Aberdeen possesses granite polishing works, all of which deserve notice. Its fine steamers and clippers, with the "Aberdeen bow," are well known.

Bradshaw's Handbook, 1863.

Monday

24

Tuesday

25

Wednesday

26

Thursday

27

Friday

28

Saturday

29

Sunday

30

Providing rail access to the most northerly parts of Scotland was the Highland Railway, picking up where the Caledonian left off, just north of Perth. This HR poster advertises the Victorian spa of Strathpeffer, the fortunes of which were transformed by the coming of the railway. (SSPL/Getty)

Early May bank holiday (UK)

Monday

1

Tuesday

2

Wednesday

3

Thursday

4

Friday

5

Saturday

6

Sunday

7

One of the three links in the great chain that was the East Coast main line between Scotland and London, was the Great Northern Railway, carrying passengers on the most southerly part of the route, between York and London. From 1870 for thirty years the glamorous queens of that company were the 'Singles' designed by Patrick Stirling. This photograph shows no. 665 leaving Boston station near the end of its distinguished career. (SSPL/Getty)

Monday
8

Tuesday
9

Wednesday
10

Thursday
11

Friday
12

Saturday
13

Sunday
14

TINTERN ABBEY - GREAT WESTERN RAILWAY

The graceful Wye, filled up to its banks, and brimming over with the tide from the Severn Sea, glides tranquilly past the orchards and fat glebe of "Holy Tynterne." On every side stands an amphitheatre of rocks, nodding with hazel, ash, birch and yew, and thrusting out from the tangled underwood high pointed crags, as it were, for ages the silent witness of that ancient Abbey and its fortunes; but removed just such a distance as to leave a fair plain in the bend of the river, for one of the most rare and magnificent structures in the whole range of ecclesiastical architecture. As you descend the road from Chepstow, the building suddenly bursts upon you, like a gigantic stone skeleton; its huge gables standing out against the sky with a mournful air of dilapidation. There is a stain upon the walls, which bespeaks a weather-beaten antiquity; and the ivy comes creeping out of the bare, sightless windows; the wild flowers and mosses cluster upon the mullions and dripstones, as if they were seeking to fill up the unglazed void with nature's own colours.

The door is opened – how beautiful the long and pillared nave – what a sweep of graceful arches, how noble the proportions, the breadth, the length and the height.

(Extracted by the author of *Bradshaw's Handbook* from *The Book of South Wales* by Charles Frederick Cliffe.)

Monday

15

Tuesday

16

Wednesday

17

Thursday

18

Friday

19

Saturday

20

Sunday

21

An engraving of Tintern Abbey in 1896, much as it would have appeared when Bradshaw's Handbook *was written.*
(Print Collector/Getty)

The writer of *Bradshaw's Handbook* considered the Monmouthshire town of Ebbw Vale to be 'not of essential importance to the general tourist', but its contribution to the economy of South Wales, to the industry of Great Britain and the world, and to the receipts of the Great Western Railway Company should not be underestimated. A centre of coal mining and steel production, Ebbw Vale was one of the most significant places in the hive of activity that was the Welsh valleys. This view of a coal mine in Ebbw Vale was taken in the 1880s for one of the then very fashionable stereoscopic postcards. (London Stereoscopic Company/Getty)

Monday

22

Tuesday

23

Wednesday

24

Thursday

25

Friday

26

Saturday

27

Sunday

28

MERTHYR - TAFF VALE RAILWAY

Merthyr Tydfil is a parliamentary borough, and great mining town, in South Wales, 21 miles from Cardiff. It stands up the Taff, among the rugged and barren-looking hills in the north-east corner of Glamorganshire, the richest county in Wales for mineral wealth. About a century ago the first iron works were established here, since which the extension has been amazingly rapid. Blast furnaces, forges, and rolling mills are scattered on all sides. Each iron furnace is about 55 feet high, containing 5,000 cubic feet; and capable of smelting 100 tons of pig-iron weekly, and as there are upwards of 50, the annual quantity of metal may be tolerably estimated; but great as that supply may seem, it is scarcely equal to the demand created for it by railways. The largest works are those belonging to Lady Guest and Messrs. Crawshay, where 3,000 to 5,000 hands are employed. At Guest's Dowlais works there are 18 or 20 blast furnaces, besides many furnaces for puddling, balling, and refining; and 1,000 tons of coal a day are consumed.

Visitors should see the furnaces by night, when the red glare of the flames produces an uncommonly striking effect. Indeed, the town is best visited at that time, for by day it will be found dirty, and irregularly built, without order or management, decent roads or footpaths, no supply of water, and no public building of the least note, except Barracks, and a vast *Poor-House*, lately finished, in the shape of a cross, on heaps of rubbish accumulated from pits and works. Cholera and fever are, of course, at home here, in scenes which would shock even the most "eminent defender of the filth," and which imperatively demand that their Lady owner should become one of the "Nightingale sisterhood" for a brief space of time. Out of 695 couples married in 1845, 1,016 persons signed with marks, one great secret of which social drawback is the unexampled rapidity with which the town has sprung up; but we do hope that proper measures will be taken henceforth by those who draw enormous wealth from working these works, to improve the conditions of the people.

Bradshaw's Handbook, 1863.

Spring bank holiday (UK)

Monday

29

Tuesday

30

Wednesday

31

Thursday

1

Friday

2

Saturday

3

Sunday

4

This detail from Lionel Walden's 1890s painting of the Dowlais steelworks in Cardiff captures much of the strange atmosphere of Victorian industrial Britain, where heavy industry, with all its noise, light and dirt, continued well beyond nightfall. The writer of *Bradshaw's Handbook* was keen to recommend such sights to the tourist. (Heritage Images/Getty)

Monday

5

Tuesday

6

Wednesday

7

Thursday

8

Friday

9

Saturday

10

Sunday

11

SWANSEA - GREAT WESTERN RAILWAY

This important seat of the *copper trade*, is also a parliamentary borough (one member), jointly with Neath, &c., and stands at the head of a fine bay, on the west side of *Glamorganshire*, 216 miles from London, by the Great Western and South Wales Railways, population, 41,606. No copper ore is found in this part of Wales, but coal being abundant, it is brought hither from Cornwall and foreign countries to be fluxed. For this purpose, six-sided calcines, 17 to 19 feet long, and oval furnaces, 11 feet long, are used in the copper works, of which eight are here, on the river Pauley, or by the sea-side; one employing 500 to 600 men. The earliest was established about 1720, after the Cornish tinners began to take notice of copper, which hitherto they had thrown away. The ore or shiff goes through various processes, such as calcining and melting, calcining the coarse metal, which leaves about one-third copper; then melting this to a fine metal, leaving three-fifths or more than half copper; calcining the fine metal; melting the same to pigs of coarse copper, which gives nine-tenths pure metal; and lastly, roasting for blistered copper and refining it into cakes for use, which are 18 inches by 12. In this way a yearly average of 20,000 tons of copper are smelted here, from the ore brought not only from Cornwall, but from America and Australia, valued at about one and a half million sterling.

Bradshaw's Handbook, 1863.

Monday

12

Tuesday

13

Wednesday

14

Thursday

15

Friday

16

Saturday

17

Father's Day

Sunday

18

Prospect of Swansea, 1850s. (SSPL/Getty)

Fish did, indeed, come from Milford Haven, from whence it was carried by the Great Western Railway to London. By the time this poster was published in the early twentieth century, the town's former importance as dockyard, ocean terminal and centre of shipbuilding had much declined. The poster is by John Hassall, also responsible for one of the most famous of all railway posters, advertising the bracing delights of Skegness by way of his 'Jolly Fisherman'. Are these two fisherfolk perhaps related? (SSPL/Getty)

Monday

19

Tuesday

20

Wednesday

21

Thursday

22

Friday

23

Saturday

24

Sunday

25

While the Great Western Railway held the keys to South Wales and its great mineral traffic, North Wales was opened up by the LNWR. Their motivation for building into Wales had more to do with access to the Irish mails at Holyhead, and the associated ocean traffic, but the company was understandably keen to promote tourism in the beautiful Welsh mountains. This poster dates from the early years of the twentieth century. (SSPL/Getty)

Monday

26

Tuesday

27

Wednesday

28

Thursday

29

Friday

30

Saturday

1

Sunday

2

THE BRITANNIA TUBULAR BRIDGE - LONDON AND NORTH WESTERN RAILWAY

—☙ • ❧—

This magnificent structure was made to carry the Chester and Holyhead Railway across the Menai Straits. Like the beautiful bridge at Conway, it is on the tubular principle, but on a much grander scale, and is one of the most ingenious, daring, and stupendous monuments of engineering skill which modern times have seen attempted. As this gigantic and amazing structure now spans the Menai, connecting the two opposite shores of Carnarvon and the Isle of Anglesey, we may justly express our admiration of it by calling it Mr. Stephenson's *chef d'oeuvre*, but this would scarcely do justice to the remarkable bridge or its great architect, we therefore think it proper to add the following details:-

The idea of carrying a railway through a vast tube, originated with Mr. Robert Stephenson. It having been found extremely difficult to construct an arch of the immense span required; and as chain bridges were not sufficiently firm for the purpose of railway traffic, Mr. Stephenson suggested the application of iron tubes to pass from pier to pier. These tubes may be described as the double barrel of a gun on an immense scale, through which the trains pass and repass, at unslackened speed, as if it were a tunnel through solid rock on land, instead of being elevated a hundred and four feet above the sea. The suggestion of Mr. Stephenson was adopted, and the Britannia Bridge now forms an imperishable monument to his fame. The construction of the bridge, however, attracted crowds of engineers and others to watch the progress of the stupendous work, and to behold the means by which Mr. Stephenson triumphed over the difficulties he had to encounter in a task of such magnitude. "They saw, day by day, with the liveliest

Stephenson's Britannia Bridge under construction: one of the principal tubular sections has been completed and is being positioned in readiness for raising by means of hydraulic jacks. (SSPL/Getty)

satisfaction, the patient putting together of the tubes, the marvellous facility with which they were floated, and the wonderful machinery by which they were elevated to the desired altitude, until the whole was completed and the first trains run through it without its deflecting more than an inch, and there it still stands, scarcely bending to the heaviest trains, stretching itself as it basks in the warmth of the noonday sun, gathering itself back under the chill of night, bending towards every gleam of sunshine, or shrinking from every passing cloud."

The Britannia Bridge takes its name from a rock which rises about the middle of the stream, and which is bare at low water. Without this advantage the erection of the pier would have been impossible, in consequence of the strength of the current and the local difficulties. The Britannia pier is built on this rock, and even with this advantage from nature the span from each of the principal piers is 463 feet; the entire length of the bridge, 1,560 feet; and the headway at high water 100 feet, which leaves sufficient room for ships to pass under. We close our description with a brief summary of the leading statistics.

It is a wrought iron tube, made of plates riveted together; 104 feet above the water, 1,513 feet long, 14 feet wide (enough for two lines of railway), 26 feet high in the middle, and 19 feet at the sides, with a total weight of 11,400 tons. The total quantity of stone contained in the bridge is 1,400,000 cubic feet; the timber used in the various scaffoldings for the masonry platforms, for the erection of the tubes, &c., was 450,000 cubic feet. The centre pier is 230 feet high; through this it passes by an opening 45 feet long, which, with 460 feet on each side, makes the main part of the bridge 965 feet long. There are two other piers of less height. At each end are carved lions, 25 feet long. Summer heat lengthens the whole fabric about a *foot*. It was begun in 1846, and the first train

At each end of the bridge there was a grand entrance, looking like the doorway into an Egyptian temple. Here, a train is about to cross the bridge, between the two great, carved lions. (SSPL/Getty)

The Britannia Bridge, soon after completion. In the background is Thomas Telford's suspension bridge of 1826 carrying the London to Holyhead road. (Universal Images Group/Getty)

went through on 5 March, 1850. The great tubes being first riveted together, were floated out on pontoons, and then raised by hydraulic presses into their place. These presses were shown at the Great Exhibition of 1851. A pillar, near Llanfair Church, is a memorial of the only accident which occurred in the prosecution of this remarkable work. From Bangor it is approached by the Belmont tunnel, 2,172 feet long.

Bradshaw's Handbook, 1863.

According to *Bradshaw's Handbook*, Kendal was notable for its 'carpet, woollen, linsey, worsted clog, comb, bobbin, fish-hook, leather, rope, woollen cord, fruit trades, and marble works'. The LNWR were more concerned to advertise its proximity to the Lake District. Neither Bradshaw nor poster make any mention of the mint cake that is its chief claim to fame today. (SSPL/Getty)

Monday

3

Tuesday

4

Wednesday

5

Thursday

6

Friday

7

Saturday

8

Sunday

9

COALS FROM NEWCASTLE - NORTH EASTERN RAILWAY

Coal, the true riches of Newcastle, was first worked here in 1260, but the produce was scanty till steam power was used in 1714. Within a circle of 8 or 10 miles, more than 50 important collieries are open, among which are the Hetton, Hartley, Wallsend, and other familiar names, employing 10,000 to 15,000 hands. High-main coal is got from a rich bed 6 feet thick, nearly 200 fathoms beneath the surface. The great northern field, of which this is the centre, covers about 500 square miles in Northumberland and Durham, and may be 1,800 feet deep. Many and various calculations have been made by practical men and geologists as to the extent of supply, but all agree that it will take some hundreds, if not thousands, of years to exhaust it.

At Painshaw and Monkwearmouth, near Sunderland, are mines 300 fathoms, or 1,800 feet, or 1/3 mile deep, the deepest in England. The coal being brought to the water side, by truck or railway, is shot through staithes into the holds of vessels, or it is carried down the river in barges or keels, and then shovelled on board. The old collier ships are clumsy, "built by the mile," as sailors say, enough being cut off for a ship each time one is wanted; but they form a nursery of first-rate seamen. Of the three million tons sent to London, one million and upwards come from Newcastle. Latterly screw steamers have been put on to expedite the delivery in the metropolitan market, and a proposal for a coal railway has been favourably entertained.

Bradshaw's Handbook, 1863.

Monday

10

Tuesday

11

Battle of the Boyne (bank holiday, NI)

Wednesday

12

Thursday

13

Friday

14

Saturday

15

Sunday

16

Bradshaw's Handbook calls Scarborough the 'most interesting marine spa in England' and for many years it had a high reputation as one of England's more exclusive seaside resorts. This poster, published by the Great Northern Railway, draws attention to some of the town's principal delights. (SSPL/Getty)

Monday

17

Tuesday

18

Wednesday

19

Thursday

20

Friday

21

Saturday

22

Sunday

23

York's first railway station was a terminus, built within the famous city walls. This classic view of York Minster from the walls taken in about 1858 includes, in the foreground, railway carriages stabled on sidings running up to the river Ouse, which crosses the view in the middle distance. (Otto Herschan/Stringer/Getty)

Monday

24

Tuesday

25

Wednesday

26

Thursday

27

Friday

28

Saturday

29

Sunday

30

LEEDS - MIDLAND RAILWAY

This great seat of the cloth trade, and actual capital of Yorkshire, stands on a hillside by the river Aire. The parish, about six or seven miles square, with its 18 or 20 townships, was formerly a moorland tract of little value, like the rest of Yorkshire, till the discovery of coal and iron enriched it by giving such a wonderful stimulus to the progress of manufactures. Several large factories and partnership mills are established in the borough, (so distinguished from the town, where there are but few); however, most of the cloth is made at home by the hand-loom weavers, a respectable and industrious class, who carry on the business of dairy farming in addition to the loom. There may be 16,000 looms thus employed in the neighbourhood, of which only one-third are in the borough. Leeds is at the extremity of the great Yorkshire manufacturing district, which ends here so suddenly that few looms are found in the north half of the borough, which is purely agricultural. The wool having been prepared by the various processes of scouring, carding, and so forth, is handed over to the weaver, who works it on his loom, and then brings it in a rough state to the market to be sold to the finisher, in the form of mixed (or coloured) cloth, and white (or undyed) cloth. Saturday is the day for sale, which lasts under strict regulations one hour only, in which short space business to a vast extent is done with expedition and quietness. The *Mixed Cloth Hall*, in Wellington Street, is a quadrangular pile, 380 feet long, by 200 broad, and contains 1,780 freehold stalls arranged in six streets. Before this hall was built, in 1758, cloth was sold in Briggate Street, and in the 17th century it was even exposed on the parapet of the old bridge (built, 1376). The White Cloth Hall, in Calls, built in 1775, is a similar structure, 300 feet long, with five streets, and about 1,200 stands.

Bradshaw's Handbook, 1863.

Monday

31

Tuesday

1

Wednesday

2

Thursday

3

Friday

4

Saturday

5

Sunday

6

Summer bank holiday (Scotland)　　　　　　　　　　　　　Monday

7

Tuesday

8

Wednesday

9

Thursday

10

Friday

11

Saturday

12

Sunday

13

The Lancashire & Yorkshire Railway was one of the busiest of all Britain's railways, operating a great density of passenger and good services in its northern, industrial territory. This idealised painting by J. Longden shows of one of the company's 4-4-0 locomotives at the head of an express train. (SSPL/Getty)

GRIMSBY DOCKS - MANCHESTER, SHEFFIELD AND LINCOLNSHIRE RAILWAY

About fifteen years have now elapsed since a far-seeing mercantile company fastened upon this spot which the sagacity of the old roving sea-kings chose to give them the command of the Humber; and there they commenced planting, in defiance of all natural obstacles, a new commercial city, to become the new *entrepôt* of the trade between western, northern and eastern Europe.

The company invaded the domain of the rolling waters, and, upon the treacherous mud, they have raised massive superstructures, and thus added nearly 140 acres of solid land to the occupation of man; and by the happy union of science, capital, and labour, have founded, the finest harbour on the eastern coast of England. The first stone was laid by Prince Albert in 1849. The New Docks present a striking example of the advantage to be derived from a union of railways, docks, and warehouses, executed under one complete plan, and worked under one management.

In constructing these works, 135 acres have been reclaimed; wharfs or quays extend 3,600 feet in length – quays traversed by railways from the main lines into sheds and warehouses. Sheds are close to the quays, 750 feet in length, and 50 feet in breadth, affording a covered area of 4,000 feet, and a vaulted warehouse 150 feet square, for free and bonded goods. All the machinery and accessories are on the newest and most perfect principles, and the arrangements for passenger traffic and light or perishable merchandise are on an equally complete scale.

The railway extends to the edge of a low-water landing stage in the outer tidal basin, where a station is built provided with accommodation for passengers, who, within the cover of the station, may be carried by trains in attendance, as goods also may, to any part of England or Scotland.

Bradshaw's Handbook, 1863.

Monday

14

Tuesday

15

Wednesday

16

Thursday

17

Friday

18

Saturday

19

Sunday

20

SHEFFIELD - MANCHESTER, SHEFFIELD AND LINCOLNSHIRE RAILWAY

This great seat of the cutlery trade is beautifully placed on the river Sheaf, where it joins the Don, among some of the most picturesque hills in the West Riding of Yorkshire, in the district of Hallamshire, and 162 ½ miles from London, by the Great Northern Railway. Its suburbs spreading mile after mile in all directions, hill and dale, and every accessible point on the slopes between being occupied by houses and villas, in endless variety, offer to the stranger new objects of pleasure at each turn, and to the residents, prospects of great extent and beauty. To one fond of the country, rambling along river, over hills and through forests to obtain some distant point of view, no matter which, Sheffield possesses almost inexhaustible attractions. Knives, forks, razors, saws, scissors, printing type, optical instruments, Britannia metal, Sheffield plate, scythes, garden implements, files, screws, other tools, stoves, fenders, as well as engines, railway springs, buffers, &c., are among the articles manufactured here – steel being the basis of nearly all; the best of which is made from iron imported from Sweden. Sheffield plate, or silver laid on copper, was discovered here by a Sheffield man, T. Bolsover, and taken up by Mr. Handcock, about 1758. The Britannia metal and German silver are both compositions imitating this plate, the manufacture of which is much promoted by the discovery of electro-plating. Rodgers' cutlery and Wilkinson's plate warehouses are among the largest; while metal foundries, vast grinding and polishing works, are dispersed in the town, and along the Porter and other streams; coal and stone are abundant.

Bradshaw's Handbook, 1863.

Monday

21

Tuesday

22

Wednesday

23

Thursday

24

Friday

25

Saturday

26

Sunday

27

The Midland Railway route from London to the north was not the most direct (though it was arguably the most scenic), and the company tried to attract passengers by innovating in matters of comfort and luxury. It was the first company to abolish second class, raising the standard for third class passengers, and making first class more affordable in the process. This Edwardian coloured photograph shows an express train, hauled by one of the company's well known 'Compound' 4-4-0 locomotives. (SSPL/Getty)

Summer bank holiday (UK, exc. Scotland)

Monday
28

Tuesday
29

Wednesday
30

Thursday
31

Friday
1

Saturday
2

Sunday
3

NOTTINGHAM - MIDLAND RAILWAY

Nottingham is situated on a rocky eminence of red sandstone, and is allowed by competent judges to be not only one of the healthiest, but also one of the most picturesque inland towns in England. The town is now rapidly increasing, and bids fair to rank among the first manufacturing towns in England, some warehouses of great architectural beauty having already made their appearance. Within the last six or seven years, a beautiful Arboretum has been opened, which, together with the delightful walks off the Mansfield Road, and others adjoining the Queen's Road, and that leading to the banks of the Trent, form pleasant sources of recreation and enjoyment. The total population of the borough is upwards of 74,693, but the industrial population in and around Nottingham, and dependent upon its trade, is nearly three times that number. Silk, cotton stockings, and bobbin-net lace are the staple manufactures. Until recently the stockings were usually worked upon frames, rented from the employers; but this, to a great extent, has been altered since the introduction of the round frames, which are now generally confined to factories. Hand and power machines are used for the net, which was invented by Heathcote in 1809. Arkwright set up here (before 1771) one of his earliest spinning machines; it was moved by horse-power. It was on the occasion of the distress among the frame-work knitters and twist hands here that Lord Byron delivered his two speeches in Parliament, in 1812 which are usually to be found in his works. In 1817 the frame-work knitters and twist hands broke out again, under the name of Luddites, and went about destroying machinery &c. The market place is one of the finest in England, and stands on an area of upwards of five acres of land, well paved, &c., at one end of which stands the *Exchange*. Here will be found most of the principal shops in the town. The second floors of these houses hang over the pavement, supported by large pillars, and form an elegant piazza.

Bradshaw's Handbook, 1863.

Monday

4

Tuesday

5

Wednesday

6

Thursday

7

Friday

8

Saturday

9

Sunday

10

The Midland & Great Northern Joint Railway, or the 'Muddle and Get Nowhere', served part of the interior of East Anglia, and specialised in holiday traffic, hence its poster here for the Norfolk Broads and the resorts on the nearby North Sea coast. (SSPL/Getty)

SEPTEMBER

Monday
11

Tuesday
12

Wednesday
13

Thursday
14

Friday
15

Saturday
16

Sunday
17

HARWICH - GREAT EASTERN RAILWAY

A sea-port, packet station, and borough town in the county of Essex, with a population of 5,070, who return two members. It is built on a peninsular point of land, close to where the rivers Stour and Orwell join the German Ocean; and from the number of maritime advantages which Harwich possesses, it has become a place of fashionable resort, especially as the scenery in its neighbourhood has considerable beauty. The Stour and Orwell are both navigable for large vessels twelve miles above the town, the one to Ipswich, the other to Manningtree. In uniting at Harwich, these rivers form a large bay on the north and west of the town. Their joint waters then proceed southward, and fall into the sea about a mile below it, in a channel from two to three miles wide, according to the state of the tide, and in which the harbour is situated. The western bank of it is formed by the tongue of land which projects towards the north, and on which the town itself stands; the eastern bank is formed by a similar projection towards the south of the opposite coast of Suffolk, and between these two promontories the harbour is completely sheltered. It is of great extent, and forms, united to the bay, a roadsted for the largest ships. Harwich derives considerable profit from its shipping trade, fisheries and annual visitors. It has hot, cold, and vapour baths, every accommodation for sea bathing, and a number of other sources of amusement. From this place Queen Isabella (1326), Edward III. (1338 and 1340), William III., George I. and II., sailed on their visits to France, Holland and Hanover. Queen Charlotte and Louis XVIII. first landed here; and from hence was embarked in 1821 the body of that much abused princess, Queen Caroline, consort of George IV.

Bradshaw's Handbook, 1863.

Monday
18

Tuesday
19

Wednesday
20

Thursday
21

Friday
22

Saturday
23

Sunday
24

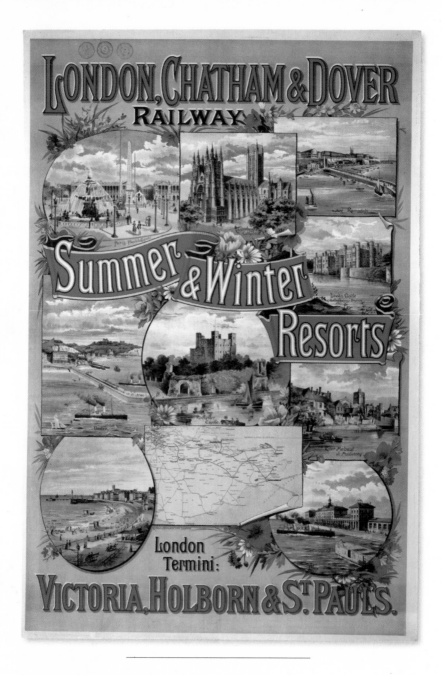

The cash-strapped London, Chatham & Dover Railway was famous for its dreadful rolling stock and poor punctuality, starting a tradition that has lasted to the present day. Its services were at their most dense in south-east London, where they coxed and boxed with those of the South Eastern Railway, but the company also served some of Kent's most glamorous leisure spots, as this 1890s poster proves. (SSPL/Getty)

Monday

25

Tuesday

26

Wednesday

27

Thursday

28

Friday

29

Saturday

30

Sunday

1

DEAL - SOUTH EASTERN RAILWAY

This old town stands close to the sea shore, which is a bold and open beach, being defended from the violence of the waves by an extensive wall of stones and pebbles which the sea has thrown up. The sea opposite the town, between the shore and the Goodwin Sands, is termed the Downs. This channel is about eight miles long and six broad, and is a safe anchorage; and in particular quarters of the wind, as many as 400 ships can ride at anchor here at one time. Deal was formerly a rough-looking, irregular, sailor-like place, full of narrow streets, with shops of multifarious articles termed slops or marine stores. It is however being much improved, and is now resorted to for sea bathing, especially on account of its good repute for moderate charges. The bathing establishment at Deal is well conducted, and there are good libraries.

It is a great pilot station for the licensed or branch pilots of the Cinque Ports; the Deal boatmen are as fine, noble and intrepid a race of seamen as any in the world, and as honest as they are brave. Deal Castle is at the south end of the town. The village of Walmer is a detached suburb of Deal, towards the south on the Dover Road. Since her majesty resided here, Walmer has been much improved and extended. It now contains several handsome villas, inhabited by a large body of gentry. The air is very salubrious, and the surrounding country pleasant and agreeable.

Walmer Castle, one of the fortresses built by Henry [VIII] in 1539, is the official residence of the Lord Warden of the Cinque Ports. It is surrounded by a moat and drawbridge. The apartments are small but convenient, and command a splendid view of the sea; but they will always have a peculiar interest for Englishmen, as having been the residence of the Duke of Wellington, and at the time which he died in 1852.

Bradshaw's Handbook, 1863.

Monday

2

Tuesday

3

Wednesday

4

Thursday

5

Friday

6

Saturday

7

Sunday

8

In the 1890s, the South Eastern Railway bought several American saloon carriages for use on its services between London and Hastings, offering a standard of luxury and spaciousness rare on British railways at that time. This 1905 poster proudly advertises this service, now operated by the South Eastern & Chatham Railway, which brought together the struggling SER and LC&DR in 1899. (SSPL/Getty)

Monday

9

Tuesday

10

Wednesday

11

Thursday

12

Friday

13

Saturday

14

Sunday

15

The coastal lines of the London, Brighton & South Coast Railway struggled to make a profit, and in an attempt to turn this situation around self-propelled steam railmotors were introduced on some services, as advertised on this early-twentieth-century poster. The venture was not a success. (SSPL/Getty)

Monday
16

Tuesday
17

Wednesday
18

Thursday
19

Friday
20

Saturday
21

Sunday
22

WEYMOUTH - LONDON SOUTH WESTERN RAILWAY

Nothing can be more striking and picturesque than the situation of this delightful watering-place. The town is built on the western shore of one of the finest bays in the English Channel, and being separated into two parts by the river, which forms a commodious harbour, it is most conveniently situated for trade. A long and handsome bridge of two arches, constructed of stone, with a swivel in the centre, was erected in 1820, and thus the divided townships enjoy a communication. The town, especially on the Melcombe side of the harbour, is regularly built, and consists chiefly of two principal streets, parallel with each other, intersected with others at right-angles; it is well paved and lighted, and is tolerably supplied with fresh water. Since the town has become a place of fashionable resort for sea-bathing, various handsome ranges of buildings, and a theatre, assembly rooms, and other places of public entertainment, have been erected, and these are now rapidly extending and increasing in every direction. From the windows of these buildings, which front the sea, a most extensive and delightful view is obtained, comprehending on the left a noble range of hills and cliffs, extending for many miles in a direction from west to east, and of the sea in front, with the numerous vessels, yachts and pleasure boats, which are continually entering and leaving the harbour.

No place can be more salubrious than Weymouth. The air is so pure and mild, that the town is not only frequented during the summer, but has been selected by many opulent families as a permanent residence; and the advantages which it possesses in the excellence of its bay, the beauty of its scenery, and the healthfulness of its climate, have contributed to raise it from the low state into which it had fallen from depression of its commerce, to one of the most flourishing towns of the kingdom.

Bradshaw's Handbook, 1863.

Monday

23

Tuesday

24

Wednesday

25

Thursday

26

Friday

27

Saturday

28

Sunday

29

BATH - GREAT WESTERN RAILWAY

_୧ • ୨_

The view from the station is one calculated to impress a stranger very favourably with the importance of the city, so renowned in the world of fashionable invalids. He sees on one side of him the river Avon, gliding placidly beneath Pulteney Bridge, and on the other a range of lofty hills, studded with terraces and isolated villas, whilst before expand the white edifices of the city.

Bath is not only renowned for its antiquity and waters, but is one of the best built cities in the United Kingdom, standing in a spot remarkable for its attractive scenery, on the Avon and the

Brunel's Tudor-style trainshed at Bath was a simplified version of the great engineer's famous, and still-extant, trainshed at Bristol Temple Meads. It was a fitting complement to the fine architecture of the rest of the city, but did not quite last into the twentieth century, being replaced by the current, more prosaic platform awnings in 1897. (SSPL/Getty)

Great Western Railway, 107 miles from London, at the centre of a fine circle of hills, 500 to 700 feet high. These hills furnish the blue lias, oolite, and Bath stone, so much in use by architects, and of which the city has been erected. It is the seat of a bishop, whose diocese extends over Somersetshire, and its population of 54,240 send two members to parliament.

The peculiar virtue of its hot-springs were soon discovered by the Romans, who built a tower here, called the *Aquae Solis* (waters of the sun), a name which, under the form of Aix, Ax, Aigs, &c., still distinguishes many watering-places on the continent. The Saxons who resorted here significantly styled one of the main roads which led to it, Akeman Strutt, i.e., the road for *aching men.*

Besides the private baths in Stall Street, there are four public ones leased from the corporation. King's Bath, the largest, a space of 65 feet by 40, with a temperature of 114°; in the middle of it a statue to "Bladud, son of Lord Hudibras, eighth king of the Britons, &c., &c., the first discoverer of these baths, 863 years B.C.," and so forth. King's Bath is in Stall Street, on one side of the colonnade and the pump-room, where the band plays. It was rebuilt in 1796, on the site of that in which Beau Nash, with a white hat for his crown, despotically ruled as master of the ceremonies in the last century. His statue is seen here by Hoare. Over the front is a Greek tee-total motto, signifying "Water is the thing." Queen's Bath, close to the other, and so called when James I.'s queen, Anne of Denmark, came here to take the waters. Hot Bath, which has a temperature of 117° (the highest), and is supplied by a spring which gives out 128 gallons per minute. Cross Bath, temperature 109°, yielding only 12 gallons a minute. This is the one recorded by Pepys in his diary, 1668. "Up at four o'clock, being by appointment called to the *Cross Bath.* By and bye much company came; very fine ladies, and the manners pretty enough, only methinks it cannot be clean to go so many bodies together in the same water. Strange to see how hot the water is;" and he wonders that those who stay the season are not all parboiled. Another bath is the property of Lord Manvers. The water is nearly transparent; about 180,000 gallons daily are given out to these baths, and this has been going on for centuries! Sulphate of lime is by far the chief ingredient; then muriate and sulphate of soda, and a little carbonic acid rising up in bubbles. They are remarkably beneficial in rheumatism, paralysis, skin complaints, scrofula, gout, indigestion, and chronic diseases of the liver, &c. House painters among others, come here to be cured of the injury done to their hands by white lead.

In this detail of a mid-nineteenth-century prospect of Bath from the south the Abbey takes centre-stage, with the Royal Cresent easily discernible at the far left. The scene is garlanded by Brunel's Great Western Railway, running across the scene in the foreground. (SSPL/Getty)

Bath is a city of terraces and crescents – viz:- the Circus, the North and South Parades, the Royal and Lansdowne Crescents, and others, either in the town or on the hills around. Some of the best buildings are by Wood, author of "Description of Bath." Among the 20 churches is the Abbey Church, or Cathedral, which replaces a monastery, founded in 970, by King Edgar; it is a cross, 240 feet long, built in the 16th century, and has 52 windows inside, with a rich one in the fine east front, and some good tracery in Prior Bird's Chapel.

St. James's is a modern Grecian church with a high tower, in Stall Street. Another church, with a fine early English spire, stands in Broad Street. St. Saviour's, at the eastern extremity of the city, and St. Stephen's, on Lansdowne, are modern Gothic churches; and several others of note. Milsom Street and Bond Street contain the best shops. Near are the Circus, and the Assembly Room, a handsome pile, built in 1771 by Wood, with a ball-room

106 feet long, and an octagon full of portraits. Another of Wood's works, the Royal Crescent, is worth notice; Smollett called it "an antique amphitheatre turned inside out." The Guildhall, a noble building in the Grecian style, is in High Street. Near at hand is a well-stocked market. Its supply of fish is very good.

Within a short distance is the General Hospital, founded chiefly through Beau Nash's exertions, for the benefit of the poor people, from all parts, using the Bath waters. Bellot's Hospital, an old building, founded in 1609. The Casualty and United Hospitals are among the various munificent institutions here. Partis's College was founded for ladies of decayed fortune. St. John's Hospital, founded in the 12th century, and rebuilt by Wood, near Cross Bath, has an income of £9,000.

There is a full and interesting museum of Roman antiquities and fossil remains at the Literary Institution, near the Baths and Parade. A club-house in York Buildings, and several public libraries.

Bradshaw's Handbook, 1863.

A TIN MINE.

Between Camborne and Redruth.

CORNWALL - CORNWALL RAILWAY

Cornwall, from its soil, appearance, and climate, is one of the least inviting of the English counties. A ridge of bare and rugged hills, intermixed with bleak moors, runs through the midst of its whole length, and exhibits the appearance of a dreary waste. The most important objects in the history of this county are its numerous mines, which for centuries have furnished employment to thousands of its inhabitants; and, the trade to which they give birth, when considered in a national point of view, is of the greatest relative consequence. In a narrow slip of land, where the purposes of agriculture would not employ above a few thousand inhabitants, the mines alone support a population estimated at more than 80,000 labourers, exclusive of artizans. The principal produce of the Cornish mines is tin, copper, and lead. The strata in which these metals are found extend from the Land's End in a direction from west to east, entirely along the country into Devonshire. Nearly all the metals are found in veins or fissures, the direction of which is generally east and west. The annual value of the copper mines has been estimated at £350,000. Logan stones deserve to be mentioned amongst the curiosities of this county. They are of great weight, and poised on the top of immense piles of rocks.

Bradshaw's Handbook, 1863.

Monday

30

Halloween   Tuesday

31

Wednesday

1

Thursday

2

Friday

3

Saturday

4

Sunday

5

A mid-nineteenth century illustration of a typical Cornish tin mine. The engine houses and chimneys in the background would have been a familiar punctuation in the landscape at this time. (Universal Images Group/Getty)

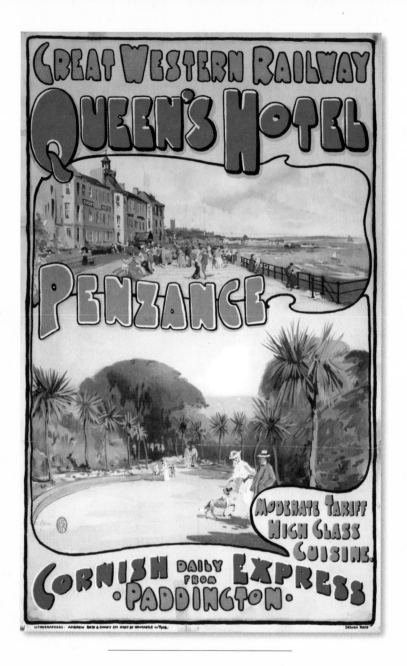

By the time this poster was published by the Great Western Railway, Cornwall was famous less as the dreary wasteland of the description in *Bradshaw*, and more a holiday paradise. Such was the power of railway companies' marketing. Here Penzance is made to appear like somewhere in the south of France; very soon afterwards, the GWR would coin the term 'Cornish Riviera' to refer to the resorts of the County's southern coast. (SSPL/Getty)

Monday

6

Tuesday

7

Wednesday

8

Thursday

9

Friday

10

Saturday

11

Sunday

12

Box Tunnel was, and remains, one of the wonders of Brunel's Great Western main line, from Bristol to London. The line was largely financed by Bristol merchants, and the structures of the line showed their grandest aspect to the traveller heading from the port city towards the capital; the eastern portal of the tunnel is seldom illustrated for reasons that become clear if you stick your head out of a train window on the approach from Chippenham. This famous illustration was made by John Bourne soon after the line opened. (SSPL/Getty)

Monday

13

Tuesday

14

Wednesday

15

Thursday

16

Friday

17

Saturday

18

Sunday

19

WOOLWICH ARSENAL - SOUTH EASTERN RAILWAY

The "Royal Arsenal" is composed of several buildings, wherein the manufacture of implements of warfare is carried on upon the most extensive scale. On entering the gateway the visitor will see the "Foundry" before him, provided with everything necessary for casting the largest pieces of ordnance, for which, as in the other branches of manufacture, steam power has lately been applied. Connected with the "Pattern Room," adjoining, will be noticed several of the illuminations and devices used in St. James's Park to commemorate the peace of 1814. The "Laboratory" exhibits a busy scene, for here are made the cartridges, rockets, fireworks, and other chemical contrivances for warfare, which, though full of "sound and fury," are far from being considered amongst the enemy as "signifying nothing." To the north are the storehouses, where are deposited outfittings for 15,000 cavalry horses, and accoutrements for service. The area of the Arsenal contains no less than 24,000 pieces of ordnance, and 3,000,000 cannon balls piled up in huge pyramids. The "Repository" and "Rotunda" are on the margin of the Common, to the south of the town, and contain models of the most celebrated fortifications in Europe, with curiosities innumerable. To the south-east of the Repository is the "Royal Military Academy," for the education of the cadets in all the branches of artillery and engineering. The present building, partly in the Elizabethan style, was erected in 1805, and though 300 could be accommodated, the number of cadets at present does not exceed 160.

The following form the arrangements for admission to the above important buildings:- To the Arsenal, the Royal Repository, and the Dockyard, *free*; the hours being from 9 till 11 a.m., and 1 till 4 p.m. Visitors are required to leave their names at the gates. The other buildings require the escort of one of the principal officers.

Bradshaw's Handbook, 1863.

Monday

20

Tuesday

21

Wednesday

22

Thursday

23

Friday

24

Saturday

25

Sunday

26

THE TOWER OF LONDON

The Tower of London, erected by William the Conqueror, connects itself with every succeeding event in the history of our race. In more barborous times than those in which we live, it has been the prison-house, and the place of execution of illustrious victims of tyranny. Perhaps there is no single spot in Europe, or in the world, so calculated to awaken impressive and profitable recollections, and so pregnant with interest to Englishmen, as this place. Within these venerable vaults, human nature has been exhibited in all its extremes. The pomp of royalty, wretchedness of solitude, horrors of murder and martyrdom, all stand associated with the eventful history of the building. The Yeomen of the Guard, better known as beefeaters, in the picturesque costume of Elizabeth, conduct the visitors over it. Within the court-yard, a number of objects are pointed out that are rich in historical interest, of the most romantic and mournful character. There stands the Bloody Tower in which the unfortunate young prince, Edward V. and his brother, are said to have been smothered by order of Richard III. The Beauchamp Tower is also shown, as the prison in which the ill-fated Anne Boleyn, and the highly gifted and unfortunate Lady Jane Grey were confined. The Armoury is one of the most extensive in the world. There is one immense room containing, it is said, two hundred thousand muskets, tastefully and beautifully arranged. On all sides are trophies of victories by land and sea, and in a noble gallery called the Horse Armoury, are arranged in complete panoply the effigies of many of England's greatest monarch warriors, clad in the very armour which they had worn. The regalia of England is preserved in a very massive strong tower, without windows, and quite dark from without, being lit by a powerful lamp, which exhibits the brilliancy and value of the precious stones. Everything is admirably arranged for exhibition; the imperial crown, and other most precious articles are turned round, so as to be seen, on all sides, by means of ingenious machinery, touched by the ancient dame who exhibits them.

Bradshaw's Handbook, 1863.

Monday

27

Tuesday

28

Wednesday

29

St Andrew's Day (bank holiday, Scotland)

Thursday

30

Friday

1

Saturday

2

Sunday

3

The North London Railway was more reliant upon passenger revenues than many, and it faced increasing competition from trams and underground lines. This Edwardian poster appeals to the commuter who valued views and fresh air more highly than speed and convenience. (SSPL/Getty)

Monday

4

Tuesday

5

Wednesday

6

Thursday

7

Friday

8

Saturday

9

Sunday

10

CRYSTAL PALACE - LONDON BRIGHTON & SOUTH COAST RAILWAY

_⟋⟍ • ⟋⟍_

The site of the Crystal Palace is one of the most beautiful in the world. Standing on the brow of the hill, some two hundred feet above the valley through which the railway passes, the building is visible for many miles in every direction. But when the train approaches the spot where the brilliant and fairy fabric, in the midst of the most enchanting scenery, is reveled suddenly to the eye, the impression produced elicits our warmest admiration. The models of the diluvian and antediluvian extinct animals, the Irish elk with its magnificently branching antlers, the two Iguanadons, the Megalosaurus, &c., in the foreground among the Geological Islands and Lakes; the cascades and terraces, the luxuriant foliage, flower-beds and fountains, ascending up to the splendid and unrivalled fabric of glass which rears its radiant and glittering bulk upon the Surrey hill, form a _coup d'oeil_ of wonderful beauty, magnificence, and grandeur, the view of which we may envy the Brighton railway traveller who enjoys the sight daily, in virtue of his season ticket.

Any one who appreciates the beautiful will always feel gratified even with a passing view; but every person who can spare the time should visit on a fete day.

Excursion trains to and from London Bridge afford every facility. The building, the grounds or park, the salubrity of the air, the waterworks, the garden inside and out, the fine art courts and collections, form a combination of attractions unsurpassed in any country.

The visitor from London is conveyed to the station of the Crystal Palace in twenty minutes. On emerging from the train he ascends the flight of stairs in the south wing and reaches the centre nave or great transept in a few moments, and immediately beholds that unrivalled view which we all admire with feelings of pride and satisfaction as the most wonderful work human hands and mind have yet achieved.

The whole of the sides of the nave and the divisions on either side are lined with plants and trees from every clime, interspersed with statues and works of art, and embellished

Crystal Palace was popular not only for the building and what it contained, but (among yet other things) for the impressive display of fountains outside. These were supplied with water under pressure by two huge water tanks, designed by Brunel, one of which is evident in this photograph. (Hulton Archive/Stringer/Getty)

with beautiful fountains in the centre. The great transept, with its trees and flowers and fountains divides the nave into two equal parts – the northern division dedicated to art, and the southern to commerce, or to the industrial display of the manufactures of the United Kingdom, which, by the way, under injudicious management is becoming not only less attractive than formerly, but quite contemptible. The transept has the appearance of a great conservatory, embellished with the finest and rarest models and *chefs d'oeuvres* of ancient and modern statuary. This series of courts represents and illustrates the architecture of ancient art.

The **Pompeian Court** is the exact fac-simile of the interior of a building discovered in the ruins of Pompeii. Mosaic pavements and walls, divided into compartments, in which mythological subjects are beautifully painted.

The **Egyptian Court** is highly suggestive of the grand and massive character of Egyptian architecture and its lion-faced Sphinxes, its solemn heads of colossal women, its gigantic figures, and its walls covered with hieroglyphs.

The **Greek Court**, containing copies of unrivalled works of sculpture, groups of great beauty, and specimens of perfect architecture.

The **Roman Court**, richly stored with Roman sculpture, models, and curious gems.

The **Alhambra Court**, representing several courts of the *famous palace* of the Moorish Kings of Granada, the Court of Lions, and Hall of Justice.

The **Assyrian and Nineveh Court**, displaying the wonders of Nineveh, with its colossal divinities, Rhea, and the gigantic Sphinxes, its eagle-winged and human-headed bulls, and its cuneiform hieroglyphics. And then on the opposite side are the several courts, in which are given illustrations of the Byzantine, Mediaeval, and Renaissance styles of architecture, including models of the French, English, German, and Italian schools, each court being complete in itself, and entered by a characteristic doorway.

Modern Picture Gallery. – In this extensive space will be found one of the best lighted and most spacious galleries of modern pictures to be found in England. These works of art have been contributed by proprietors, and also by artists,

The interior of the Crystal Palace, as rebuilt at Sydenham. Although using many of the structural components of the original Crystal Palace of 1851, the building was in fact significantly redesigned before being re-erected. (SSPL/Getty)

ENGLISH VIEWS

and many of them are deposited here for sale. Thus this portion of the building combines the attractions of private collections and public exhibitions, with the additional advantage, that only the best works of art are accepted for exhibition.

On leaving the central transept the visitor descends a flight of granite steps leading to the Upper Terrace, which extends within the two advancing wings of the palace, and commands a splendid view of the gardens, and of the whole country beyond the railway, to the summit of the Surrey hills.

The Terrace Garden is adorned with a central circular basin, throwing out a *Jet d'Eau*, besides others of an elliptical shape. At the extremity of each wing there is a tower in the form of a Greek Cross, which have each on their summit a tank, containing 924 tons of water, to be distributed for any purposes throughout the building. The high towers, of which there are two, one at each end of the building, have been erected for the purpose of carrying the tanks that supply the fountains in the lower basin, and are, with the exception of the tank and stays, constructed of cast-iron.

Flights of steps lead to the Italian and Flower Garden and Terrace below, and to a series of basins and caves, receiving fountains, and waterfalls, containing six times the amount of water thrown up by the Grand Eaux at Versailles.

Along the great walk the water of the upper basin flows down in a series of cascades, until it falls into an open colonnade, and then rushes into falls on each side of the walk, half a mile in length, which supply numerous other fountains.

On ordinary occasions the basins and fountains give life and freshness to the garden, but on fete days the vast waters are unloosed, and rushing upwards in a thousand streams, or dashing over the colonnades, make the whole garden ring with their tumultuous murmerings, producing a magnificent effect, a splendid brilliancy in the sunbeam, joined to the fragrance and freshness of the flowers, of which few can form a conception who have not witnessed it. One of the most curious features of the Palace is the Geological Islands, and the specimens of the extinct animals, life-like gigantic models of which are distributed over the islands and lakes.

There is a splendid Refreshment Room for the first class visitors, where parties can have hot dinners served in a first-rate style, at not unreasonable prices.

KING'S CROSS STATION - GREAT NORTHERN RAILWAY

The terminus for the passenger and goods traffic of the Great Northern Railway at King's Cross presents a most imposing appearance. In the *façade*, the two main arches mark the end of the arrival and departure platforms, and each have a span of no less than 71 feet.

Three large doorways admit passengers, on their arrival with their luggage, into the booking office. Convenient and spacious apartments, right and left of it, accommodate passengers until the trains are about to start, when they pass on to the platforms. Near the first-class waiting room, and to the platform where it communicates, is an excellent refreshment and coffee room.

On reaching the platform the traveller cannot fail to admire the size and character of the station, the semi-spherical roof, the immense area covered in, and the general arrangement to afford accommodation for several distinct lines of railway.

The goods station of this terminus covers a surface of ground of about 45 acres, laid out for the receiving, sorting and dispatching of minerals, merchandise, and produce of every kind from every place, and to any destination, communicating with the railway, and is situated in Maiden Lane, Battle Bridge, north of the Regent's Canal, by which it is bounded on two sides, and from which water-communications are made to the docks constructed in the station. In the whole of the buildings Mr. Lewis, the architect, sought to combine with the greatest strength and cheapness of construction the utmost facilities for the transit and stowage of goods.

The Granary, which fronts the canal dock is 70 feet high, has six stories, 180 by 100 feet, and will hold 60,000 sacks of corn.

The goods-shed, the largest of its kind in the kingdom, is of brick, 600 feet in length, 80 feet wide, and 25 feet high. It is a model warehouse, complete with platforms, railway trucks, wagons, cranes, canal; and the ease and rapidity with which goods can be laden or unladen, lifted from the canal or shipped in barges, is extraordinary.

Bradshaw's Handbook, 1863.

Monday

11

Tuesday

12

Wednesday

13

Thursday

14

Friday

15

Saturday

16

Sunday

17

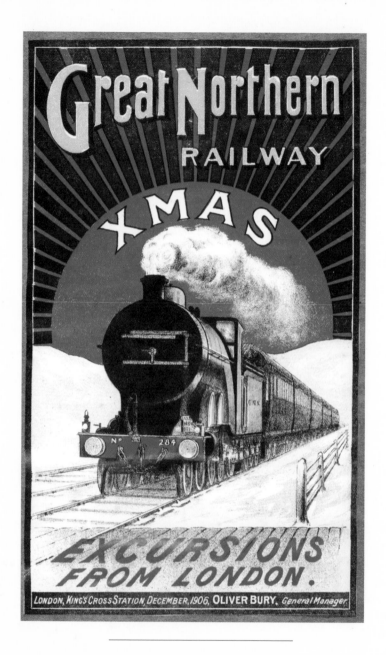

This cheerful brochure cover of 1905, promoting Christmas excursions, uses an image of one of the Great Northern Railway's brand new 'Large Atlantic' locomotives. So named for its 4-4-2 wheel arrangement, and its large boiler and wide firebox, these engines were the mainstay of fast express services on the East Coast main line until the coming of Gresley's 'Pacifics' in the 1920s. (SSPL/Getty)

Monday
18

Tuesday
19

Wednesday
20

Thursday
21

Friday
22

Saturday
23

Sunday
24

The end of the line. This early (and probably imaginary) view of a snowy train arrived at its destination includes two horse-drawn carriages on trucks coupled to the end of the train. The carriage of private vehicles in this way was common practice until increasing traffic and pressure to turn passenger trains around quickly made it a rare sight on the main line. (SSPL/Getty)

Christmas Day (bank holiday, UK)

Monday

25

Boxing Day (bank holiday, UK)

Tuesday

26

Wednesday

27

Thursday

28

Friday

29

Saturday

30

New Year's Day

Sunday

31